Growing in C H R I S T *Series*

A 13-WEEK COURSE FOR
NEW AND GROWING CHRISTIANS

NAVPRESS

Discipleship Inside Out™

NavPress is the publishing ministry of The Navigators, an international Christian organization and leader in personal spiritual development. NavPress is committed to helping people grow spiritually and enjoy lives of meaning and hope through personal and group resources that are biblically rooted, culturally relevant, and highly practical.

For a free catalog go to www.NavPress.com
or call 1.800.366.7788 in the United States or 1.800.839.4769 in Canada.

© 1957, 1975, 1980, 2007 by The Navigators

All rights reserved. No part of this publication may be reproduced in any form without written permission from NavPress, P.O. Box 35001, Colorado Springs, CO 80935. www.navpress.com

NAVPRESS and the NAVPRESS logo are registered trademarks of NavPress. Absence of * in connection with marks of NavPress or other parties does not indicate an absence of registration of those marks.

ISBN-13: 978-0-89109-157-8

Cover design by Tim Green, The DesignWorks Group, www.thedesignworksgroup.com
Creative Team: Darla Hightower, Arvid Wallen, Pat Reinheimer

Unless otherwise identified, all Scripture quotations in this publication are taken from the HOLY BIBLE: NEW INTERNATIONAL VERSION* (NIV*). Copyright © 1973, 1978, 1984 by International Bible Society. Used by permission of Zondervan Publishing House. All rights reserved. Also, Scripture quotations on the enclosed verse cards are from the HOLY BIBLE: NEW INTERNATIONAL VERSION* (NIV*). Copyright © 1973, 1978, 1984 by International Bible Society. Used by permission of Zondervan Publishing House. All rights reserved; the *King James Version* (KJV); the *New American Standard Bible* (NASB), © The Lockman Foundation 1960, 1962, 1963, 1968, 1971, 1972, 1973, 1975, 1977, 1995; and the *New Revised Standard Version* (NRSV), copyright © 1989, by the Division of Christian Education of the National Council of the Churches of Christ in the USA, used by permission, all rights reserved.

Printed in the United States of America

5 6 7 8 9 10 / 13 12 11 10

INTRODUCTION

Jesus Christ said, "Here I am! I stand at the door and knock. If anyone hears my voice and opens the door, I will come in and eat with him, and he with me" (Revelation 3:20). Coupled with this wonderful truth is the statement in the gospel of John that "to all who received him, to those who believed in his name, he gave the right to become children of God" (John 1:12).

If you have to the best of your knowledge received Jesus Christ, God's Son, as your own Savior, according to the Scriptures quoted above you have become a child of God.

Too many people make the mistake of measuring the certainty of their salvation by their feelings. Don't make this tragic mistake. Believe God! Take Him at His word: "I write these things to you who believe in the name of the Son of God so that you may know that you have eternal life" (1 John 5:13).

It is impossible in the short space of this book to go into all the results of the transaction that took place when you received Christ. A child may be born into a wealthy home and become the possessor of good parents, brothers and sisters, and houses and lands; but at the time of his birth it is not necessary that he be informed of all these things. There are more important matters to take care of first. He must be protected, for he has been born into a world of many enemies. In the hospital room he is handled with sterilized gloves and kept from outsiders that he might not fall victim to countless germs waiting to attack. He must be given nourishment regularly, and protected from exposure to extreme heat or cold.

You have become a child of God; you have been born into His family as a spiritual babe. You have the potential to live the rest of your life in victorious obedience to God. It is our desire to share with you a few simple truths that will strengthen you and keep you safe from the onslaughts of Satan.

In 1 Peter 2:2 you will read, "Like newborn babies, crave pure spiritual milk, so that by it you may grow up in your salvation." And in Acts 20:32 you will read, "Now I commit you to God and to the word of his grace, which can build you up." His Word will now serve as your spiritual food and will build you up in the faith.

You probably have a Bible. If not, get one and begin to read it faithfully every day. It is important that you begin to set aside time, preferably in the morning, to read and study the Word of God, and to pray. A good place to start reading would be the gospel of John or the gospel of Mark.

A very effective way to get the Bible into your life is to begin memorizing key portions of it. Why should we do this? In Psalm 119:9 we read, "How can a young man keep his way pure? By living according to your word." Then in verse 11 the psalmist says to the Lord, "I have hidden your word in my heart that I might not sin against you." God's Word gives us answers to everyday problems. So we challenge you to hide His Word in your heart — to memorize it — to become stronger in your Christian life. This course includes thirteen key memory passages for you to learn.

But first, let us consider the new enemy you now face. Before you trusted Christ, Satan may not have bothered you particularly. But now you have left his crowd and joined the ranks of those who believe in and follow the Son of God and His Word. You are no longer in Satan's domain. You now belong to Christ who has bought and paid for you with a price — the price of His own blood shed on the cross. You may be sure that Satan will attempt to trouble you.

We can overcome Satan only as we use the weapons God has provided. In Ephesians 6:17 we read, "Take the helmet of salvation and the sword of the Spirit, which is the word of God." The Word of God is the sword of the Spirit — our weapon of offense. In verse 16 of this chapter we are also commanded to "take up the shield of faith, with which you can extinguish all the flaming arrows of the evil one." Faith is our shield. And so, since the Word of God is the source of our faith, the Scriptures are also our weapon of defense.

In Matthew 4:1-11 you can read how Jesus Christ Himself was tempted by Satan in three specific ways. Jesus defeated him each time by quoting Scripture, submitting Himself to its authority. If Christ deemed it necessary to meet Satan this way how much more do we need this mighty weapon, the Word of God, in our battles with evil!

PART 1

LESSONS ON ASSURANCE

To assure is to "put beyond all doubt." *Lessons on Assurance* will help to assure you or "put you beyond all doubt" regarding some basic promises God has made to Christians. You can become convinced of the reality of these promises in your life as you memorize, meditate on, study, and apply the Scripture verses presented here.

Always memorize the verse presented at the beginning of each lesson. (Use the verse cards in the back of this booklet.) You may want to begin by memorizing the verse, or you may prefer to do the study questions about the verse first. In either case, be sure to memorize the topic and the reference as well as the verse. (The topic for each verse is the same as the lesson title in this book.)

One good way to memorize these is to quote the topic and reference at the beginning of the verse, and the reference at the end of the verse. For example, in quoting the verse in Lesson 1 you would say, "Assurance of Salvation, First John five, eleven and twelve," and then repeat the verse. At the end you would repeat the reference again.

Learn one phrase at a time. Say, "Assurance of Salvation, First John five, eleven and twelve, 'And this is the testimony . . .'" Repeat this several times until you know it. Then, repeating what you have just learned, add the next phrase: "Assurance of Salvation, First John five, eleven and twelve, 'And this is the testimony: God has given us eternal life . . .'" Repeat all of this several times until you know it. Then add the next phrase. Repeat the process until you have memorized the verse.

In the back of this workbook are Scripture memory cards

containing thirteen verses or passages from the *King James Version*, the *New International Version*, the *New American Standard Bible*, and the *New Revised Standard Version*.

An essential part of Scripture memory is review. Review, review, review! This will help you retain what you have memorized. Be sure to review each verse daily. You can take advantage of spare moments by carrying the verse cards you have learned wherever you go.

In each lesson you will:

- Memorize a verse.
- Think over what the verse says and means, and answer questions about it.
- Study other related passages.
- Write out the verse from memory.
- Write out a way to apply the verse to your everyday life.

Going through this process of memorizing, meditating, studying, and applying will help you understand and live by the principles presented in the verses.

1

ASSURANCE OF SALVATION

> **MEMORIZE 1 JOHN 5:11-12**
> *Assurance of Salvation*
>
> And this is the testimony: God has given us eternal life,
> and this life is in his Son. He who has the Son has life; he
> who does not have the Son of God does not have life.
>
> 1 JOHN 5:11-12

The five verses you will memorize and study in *Lessons on Assurance* will equip you for your first encounters with the enemy. His first approach is often to cast doubt on the work God has done in your heart. Although you won't hear his audible voice, he will whisper this in your mind:

"You don't think you are saved and your sins forgiven just by believing and receiving Christ? Surely that is not enough!"

What will your answer be? Your only hope of successfully resisting such an attack is to resort to God's Word. What does God say about the matter? That is the important thing for you to know.

On the basis of this "testimony" — God's written Word — you can be convinced you have the Lord Jesus Christ, and with Him eternal life. You can thus overcome in this first test of your faith. The attack may recur, but now you can meet it with the Word of God in your heart.

EXPLORING 1 JOHN 5:11-12
Who gives eternal life?

Where is eternal life found?

Who has eternal life?

Who does not have eternal life?

"THIS IS THE TESTIMONY"
1. What did John say in John 20:31 about why he wrote this book?

"GOD HAS GIVEN US ETERNAL LIFE"
2. According to Romans 5:8, how has God shown that He loves you?

3. What results of man's sinfulness are listed in Isaiah 59:2?

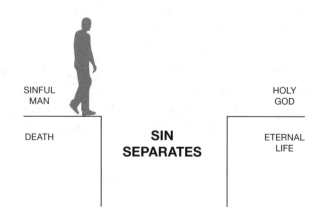

SINFUL MAN   HOLY GOD

DEATH   **SIN SEPARATES**   ETERNAL LIFE

4. Read Ephesians 2:8-9. Why do human efforts always fail to reach God?

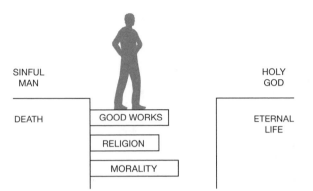

5. In 1 Peter 3:18, how did Peter explain what God has done to bring men to Himself?

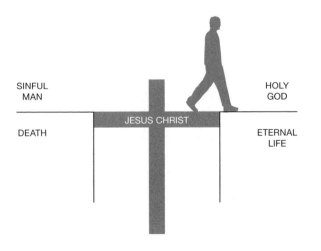

6. How did John say a person receives the gift of salvation in John 1:12?

"He Who Has the Son Has Life"

7. According to John 5:24, what three things are the result of hearing and believing?

Present

Future

Past

8. What did Jesus promise His followers in John 10:27-29?

9. What takes place when a person becomes a Christian, as described in 2 Corinthians 5:17?

Which of the following changes have you experienced in your life? (Check appropriate ones.)

☐ Inner peace
☐ New awareness of sin
☐ Victory over sin

- ☐ New love for God
- ☐ Desire to read the Bible
- ☐ Attitude changes
- ☐ Sense of forgiveness
- ☐ New concern for others

WRITE OUT 1 JOHN 5:11-12 FROM MEMORY.

APPLYING 1 JOHN 5:11-12

Meditate on 1 John 5:11-12 and consider how to apply it to your life. How do you know that you have eternal life?

Now take a few moments to thank God for all He has given you in Jesus Christ.

2

ASSURANCE OF ANSWERED PRAYER

Review 1 John 5:11-12, and check here ☐ after quoting it correctly from memory.

> ### MEMORIZE JOHN 16:24
> *Assurance of Answered Prayer*
>
> "Until now you have not asked for anything in my name. Ask and you will receive, and your joy will be complete."
>
> JOHN 16:24

Another attack of Satan may be to cause you to doubt the effectiveness of prayer. He may whisper to you, "You don't think God is personally interested in you? He's far away, and concerned about more important things. Surely you don't think He'll hear your prayers — much less answer them!"

But with Jesus Christ as your Savior and Lord, you have the unique privilege of speaking directly with your heavenly Father through Him. God wants you to come confidently into His presence through Christ and to talk to Him about everything (see Philippians 4:6 and Hebrews 4:14-16). He is intensely interested in you and your needs.

In the memory verse for this lesson, John 16:24, Jesus was speaking to His disciples the night before His crucifixion. He did not tell them they had never before asked for anything in prayer. But He said they had not asked *in His name*. You yourself have probably prayed many times, especially when in trouble. But as a believer in Christ you can ask in Jesus' name, because you belong to Him. To ask in His name means to ask in His authority and on His merit. Just as the Father answered Jesus' every prayer, so He will answer you when you ask in Jesus' name.

Memorize this promise, apply its truth, and experience the joy of answered prayer.

EXPLORING JOHN 16:24

What is prayer?

In whose name should you pray?

What results from prayer?

"UNTIL NOW YOU HAVE NOT ASKED FOR ANYTHING IN MY NAME"

1. What does Jesus teach about prayer in Matthew 7:7-8?

2. What are some important conditions for answered prayer?
   John 15:7

   1 John 5:14-15

3. What is characteristic of God's answers to prayer?
   Jeremiah 33:3

   Ephesians 3:20

4. Read Matthew 7:9-11. What kind of gifts does God give His children?

   How do you think God would respond to a request for something
   He knew would be bad for you?

   What do you think God would do if He knew the answer would be
   better for you at another time?

5. Read Philippians 4:6-7. What is the wrong reaction to have toward
   difficult circumstances?

   What is the right response?

   What is the result of this right response?

"Your Joy Will Be Complete"

6. From Philippians 4:7, what results from the peace that comes
   through prayer?

7. Read Luke 1:13-14. What resulted when Zechariah and Elizabeth prayed for a son?

8. What are some hindrances to answered prayer?
James 4:3

Psalm 66:18

WRITE OUT JOHN 16:24 FROM MEMORY.

Four important areas of prayer are:

ADORATION	— reflecting on God Himself. Praise Him for His love, His power and majesty, and His wonderful gift of Christ.
CONFESSION	— admitting your sins to God. Be honest and humble. Remember He knows you and loves you still.
THANKSGIVING	— telling God how grateful you are for everything He has given — even the unpleasant things. Your thankfulness will help you see His purposes.
SUPPLICATION	— making specific requests, both for others and for yourself.

The first letters of these four words form the word "ACTS." Use this as a mental guide for a balanced prayer life.

APPLYING JOHN 16:24

List four specific things you can pray about today. Pause right now and talk to God about them.

Adoration

Confession

Thanksgiving

Supplication

3

ASSURANCE OF VICTORY

Review the following verses, and check them off after quoting them correctly from memory.

☐ 1 John 5:11-12   ☐ John 16:24

> ### MEMORIZE 1 CORINTHIANS 10:13
> *Assurance of Victory*
>
> No temptation has seized you except what is common to man. And God is faithful; he will not let you be tempted beyond what you can bear. But when you are tempted, he will also provide a way out so that you can stand up under it.
>
> 1 CORINTHIANS 10:13

Still another attack from Satan may be along this line: He will whisper to you, "You have life, all right, but you are a weakling; you have always been a weakling."

He will remind you of some sin which has gripped you for years. He will point to something of which you are keenly aware, and say, "You are weak, and you will not be able to stand against this temptation. You may be able to stand against others, but not this one."

How will you answer him? Will you attempt to reason? Will you try to produce your own arguments? Will you run to see what other people say? Or will you resort to the invincible Word of God?

Knowing 1 Corinthians 10:13 will allow you to ward off this attack. God promises victory. It belongs to you as His child. Believe Him, and you will see how God does things that are impossible with men. It will thrill you to see chains of lifetime habits broken by His mighty power.

EXPLORING 1 CORINTHIANS 10:13

What is true about every temptation you face?

Who can give you victory when you are tempted?

Does God remove temptation?

What does God do for you?

"TEMPTATION . . . IS COMMON TO MAN"

1. What is a major source of temptation that James described in James 1:13-14?

2. Read 1 John 2:15-16. What are three primary areas of temptation?

3. According to Peter's statement in 1 Peter 5:8, what is the Devil seeking to do when he tempts you?

What does this mean to you?

"GOD IS FAITHFUL"

4. What does God do for you, according to 2 Thessalonians 3:3?

5. What does Hebrews 4:15 tell you about Jesus Christ?

"A WAY OUT"

6. What are some things you can do to keep temptation from leading into sin?
Matthew 6:9,13

Psalm 119:9,11

1 John 5:4-5

Hebrews 4:16

James 4:7

WRITE OUT 1 CORINTHIANS 10:13 FROM MEMORY.

APPLYING 1 CORINTHIANS 10:13

What is a temptation that frequently seizes you?

What do you think God's way of escape is?

4

Assurance of Forgiveness

Review the following verses, and check them off after quoting them correctly from memory.

☐ 1 John 5:11-12   ☐ 1 Corinthians 10:13
☐ John 16:24

> **MEMORIZE 1 JOHN 1:9**
> *Assurance of Forgiveness*
>
> If we confess our sins, he is faithful and just and will forgive us our sins and purify us from all unrighteousness.
>
> 1 JOHN 1:9

Although victory over sin is rightfully yours, there will be times when you miss the way of escape. You will fail and sin against God. Once you do, your enemy will be on the job immediately:

"Now you've done it. Aren't you supposed to be a Christian? Christians don't do those things."

But God makes provision in His Word for the failures of His children, as we see in 1 John 1:9. We receive His full forgiveness as we confess to Him our sins.

To confess a sin means to uncover it and call it exactly what God calls it. This honest confession must include the willingness to forsake the sin. God promises not only to forgive us, but also to cleanse us from all unrighteousness. What a gracious provision!

EXPLORING 1 JOHN 1:9
What does God want you to do about your sins?

What does it mean to confess?

In His act of forgiving us, how is God described?

What else does God do when you confess your sins?

"IF WE CONFESS OUR SINS"
1. Read 1 John 1:8,10. What did John say you should recognize about yourself?

2. What should be your attitude toward sin?
   Psalm 139:23-24

   Psalm 38:18

3. What should accompany your confession of sin, according to Proverbs 28:13?

4. How is God described in Psalm 86:5?

5. According to Ephesians 1:7, on what basis are you forgiven?

6. What does Hebrews 10:12 say about Christ's sacrifice?

7. Read Hebrews 10:17. Why is it foolish for you to continue to feel guilty about sin?

8. According to Ephesians 4:32, what should be your attitude toward those who have offended you? Why?

Write Out 1 John 1:9 from Memory.

Applying 1 John 1:9

Perhaps as you worked on this lesson something came to your mind which is hindering your fellowship with God — some sin you have committed for which you have not asked forgiveness. If so, write down what God brought to your mind.

Confess this to God, and claim the promise of 1 John 1:9 that He has forgiven your sin. Thank Him for His forgiveness.

5

Assurance of Guidance

Review the following verses, and check them off after quoting them correctly from memory.

- ☐ 1 John 5:11-12
- ☐ John 16:24
- ☐ 1 Corinthians 10:13
- ☐ 1 John 1:9

> **MEMORIZE PROVERBS 3:5-6**
>
> *Assurance of Guidance*
>
> Trust in the LORD with all your heart and lean not on your own understanding; in all your ways acknowledge him, and he will make your paths straight.
>
> PROVERBS 3:5-6

You may have questions about the future, wondering how this new life of yours is going to work out. What about God's will for your life? Will He really lead you?

God does promise to lead you as you rely on Him completely. He can guide you perfectly, for He knows all your needs, and has infinite wisdom, power, and riches to give you the best life possible.

He deserves your trust.

EXPLORING PROVERBS 3:5-6

What three things are you told to do?

When these conditions are met, what are you promised?

"TRUST IN THE LORD"

1. Read Psalm 32:8. What can you trust God to do for you?

2. According to Romans 12:1-2, what steps should be taken to experience God's will?

How is God's will described?

3. To whom does God promise special blessing in Jeremiah 17:7?

"LEAN NOT ON YOUR OWN UNDERSTANDING"

4. What warning does God give in Jeremiah 17:5?

5. Read Isaiah 55:8-9. Why should we not limit ourselves to human understanding?

6. What principle, described in John 6:38, did Jesus follow in making decisions?

"IN ALL YOUR WAYS ACKNOWLEDGE HIM"
7. List some of the "ways" of your life in which you need to acknowledge God (for example: spending money, your job, leisure time).

Select one of them, and tell how you can better acknowledge God in this area.

"HE WILL MAKE YOUR PATHS STRAIGHT"
8. What means has God provided for determining His will?

Psalm 119:105

1 Corinthians 2:12

9. Read James 1:5. What should you do about situations you don't understand?

How are you to ask? (See James 1:6-7.)

10. What precedes the fulfillment of God's promises, according to Hebrews 10:36?

WRITE OUT PROVERBS 3:5-6 FROM MEMORY.

APPLYING PROVERBS 3:5-6
Describe a situation in your life in which you are seeking God's guidance.

List ways that show how you can trust God in this situation.

PART 2

LESSONS ON CHRISTIAN LIVING

As you grow in the Christian life it is important to continue studying the Bible regularly and learning how to practice the basics of Christian living. In *Lessons on Christian Living* you will learn about eight principles and promises God has given you as His son or daughter, and the corresponding responsibilities and privileges you have in living a life that pleases God.

You may find it best to take a few of the study questions each day, rather than trying to do the entire lesson in one sitting. This will help you have a regular intake of the Word of God. And remember to use spare moments each day for reviewing your verses. Master each memory verse perfectly, word for word.

For effective Bible study it is helpful to have an easy-to-read Bible, a dictionary, and a quiet place to study.

6

PUTTING CHRIST FIRST

Review the following verses, and check them off after quoting them correctly from memory.

☐ 1 John 5:11-12 ☐ 1 John 1:9
☐ John 16:24 ☐ Proverbs 3:5-6
☐ 1 Corinthians 10:13

> **MEMORIZE MATTHEW 6:33**
>
> *Putting Christ First*
>
> "But seek first his kingdom and his righteousness, and all these things will be given to you as well."
>
> MATTHEW 6:33

God has given us many privileges. But we also have certain responsibilities. The Bible tells us what God expects of us. Our response should be to obey Him and to thank Him for all He has done for us.

Many promises in the Bible are unconditional. But most of those which concern our growth as Christians are conditional upon our obedience to His will. *Lessons on Christian Living* highlights eight of these responsibilities, which will help you build the foundation for a healthy Christian life.

Who will you live your life for? What has first place in your thoughts and plans? Jesus often challenged His disciples to consider their commitment to Him and His kingdom. He said, "If anyone would come after me, he must deny himself and take up his cross daily and follow me. For whoever wants to save his life will lose it, but whoever loses his life for me will save it" (Luke 9:23-24).

Following Him in this way may mean struggles and trials, but also the privilege of resting in Christ: "Come to me," Jesus said, "all you who are weary and burdened, and I will give you rest. Take my yoke upon you and learn from me, for I am gentle and humble in heart, and you will find rest for your souls. For my yoke is easy and my burden is light" (Matthew 11:28-30).

As you memorize and apply Matthew 6:33, seek to know Christ better every day. As you put Him, His will, and His work first in your daily life, you will begin to fully experience God's love and care, for He has promised to provide all of your daily needs.

EXPLORING MATTHEW 6:33
What are "these things"? (Look up Matthew 6:25-32.)

Are these necessities or luxuries? Explain your answer.

What has God promised to do if you put His interests first in your life?

"SEEK FIRST HIS KINGDOM AND HIS RIGHTEOUSNESS"
 1. What does God want us to do?
    Psalm 37:3

Psalm 37:4

Psalm 37:5

2. From 1 Samuel 12:24, give one reason for serving the Lord with all your heart.

3. Read 1 Samuel 15:22. What does God desire more than sacrifice?

4. How should we obey God's commands, according to these verses?
Psalm 119:34

Psalm 119:60

5. In 2 Timothy 3:16, what did Paul say is God's means for training us in righteousness?

"All These Things Will Be Given to You as Well"

6. Read Ephesians 3:20-21. How much do you think God can do for you?

7. In Isaiah 40:11, how does God promise to treat His people?

8. Read Philippians 4:4 and 4:6. List two things we are instructed to practice as believers.

9. How does Philippians 4:7 describe the result of applying Philippians 4:4 and 4:6?

10. What was Paul's attitude toward his circumstances in Philippians 4:11-13?

   How was he able to do this?

11. According to Matthew 6:8, how well does God know your present needs?

WRITE OUT MATTHEW 6:33 FROM MEMORY.

APPLYING MATTHEW 6:33

Take a moment to pray that God will help you give His kingdom and His righteousness first priority in all areas of your life.

From Matthew 6:25-32, list any needs that you want to trust God for. Claim His promise in Matthew 6:33 for meeting these needs, and pray about them. Place a check here when you have done this: ☐.

7

His Strength

Review the following verses, and check them off after quoting them correctly from memory.

- ☐ 1 John 5:11-12
- ☐ John 16:24
- ☐ 1 Corinthians 10:13

- ☐ 1 John 1:9
- ☐ Proverbs 3:5-6
- ☐ Matthew 6:33

MEMORIZE PHILIPPIANS 4:13

His Strength

I can do everything through him who gives me strength.

PHILIPPIANS 4:13

Occasionally you may experience failure and discouragement. But the Scriptures remind us of the Christian's true source of strength. Paul recorded God's promise this way: "My grace is sufficient for you, for my power is made perfect in weakness" (2 Corinthians 12:9).

Centuries ago, God told His people, "Do not fear, for I am with you; do not be dismayed, for I am your God. I will strengthen you and help you; I will uphold you with my righteous right hand" (Isaiah 41:10). This promise is just as sure for us today.

In all the trials and challenges you face, God's presence can sustain you.

We see this promise of God's strength throughout Scripture, as in

Proverbs 18:10: "The name of the LORD is a strong tower; the righteous run to it and are safe."

As you memorize Philippians 4:13, boldly claim the Lord's strength for every challenge and opportunity in your daily life, and watch Him work.

EXPLORING PHILIPPIANS 4:13
List some things you face which you cannot do apart from Christ's strength.

According to this verse, how should you approach these things?

"I CAN DO EVERYTHING"
1. Read 1 Corinthians 1:26-31. Why does God often choose "ordinary" people to accomplish great things for Him?

2. According to John 15:5, what can we accomplish apart from Christ?

What prerequisite for bearing fruit is mentioned in John 15:5?

3. What additional requirement for bearing fruit is listed in John 15:7?

4. Read 2 Corinthians 12:9. Should we ever allow a weakness or an inability to cause lasting discouragement?

Why not?

5. What did Paul thank God for in 2 Corinthians 2:14?

6. What three gifts from God are listed in 2 Timothy 1:7?

"Through Him Who Gives Me Strength"
7. How did Moses describe the Lord in Exodus 15:2?

8. Read Nehemiah 8:10. According to Nehemiah, what is our source of strength?

9. How did David describe the Lord in Psalm 18:1?

From Psalm 18:2, list the reasons why David thought of God as a source of strength.

10. According to Romans 5:8, what did Christ do for us when we were still sinners?

11. Read Ephesians 3:16-19. How does God strengthen us?

What is the result of this strengthening process?

12. Read 2 Timothy 4:16-18. Why did the Lord strengthen Paul?

What confidence did Paul gain as a result of this experience?

WRITE OUT PHILIPPIANS 4:13 FROM MEMORY.

APPLYING PHILIPPIANS 4:13
List one activity, project, or task in the next week in which you will need to consciously claim the promise of Philippians 4:13, and actively rely upon Christ's strength.

8

GOD'S WORD

Review the following verses, and check them off after quoting them correctly from memory.

☐ 1 John 5:11-12　　　☐ Proverbs 3:5-6
☐ John 16:24　　　　　☐ Matthew 6:33
☐ 1 Corinthians 10:13　☐ Philippians 4:13
☐ 1 John 1:9

> **MEMORIZE PSALM 119:9,11**
> *God's Word*
>
> How can a young man keep his way pure? By living according to your word. . . . I have hidden your word in my heart that I might not sin against you.
>
> PSALM 119:9,11

By having the Scriptures in our heart we can experience victory over sin, and can please God in all areas of life.

As the apostle Paul said farewell to believers from Ephesus, he committed them to God's care and reminded them that God's Word "can build you up and give you an inheritance among all those who are sanctified" (Acts 20:32). The Scriptures give us food for spiritual maturity, and prepare us for our eternity with God.

Not having a regular intake of Scripture will stunt our spiritual growth as surely as improper nourishment harms a child. "Like newborn babies," the apostle Peter wrote, "crave pure spiritual milk, so that by it you may grow up in your salvation" (1 Peter 2:2).

As you memorize Psalm 119:9,11, meditate on the ways God's Word can build you up, and look for evidence in your life of how He is doing this.

EXPLORING PSALM 119:9,11
How can you live a pure life?

What will keep you from sin?

"HOW CAN A YOUNG MAN KEEP HIS WAY PURE?"
1. Read 2 Timothy 3:16-17. What will the Scriptures do in your life?

   What will be the end result of what Scripture does in your life?

2. Read Psalm 1:1-3. Whose counsel should you avoid?

   What attitude should you have toward God's Word?

   How will your life be influenced by God's Word?

3. What does Joshua 1:8 teach us to do to live according to God's Word?

4. What did the psalmist ask God in Psalm 119:18?

5. According to verse 93, what had God's precepts done for the writer of Psalm 119?

"I Have Hidden Your Word in My Heart"

6. Read Psalm 19:7-8 and fill in the following chart.

Verse	What God's Word Is	What His Word Does
7		
7		
8		
8		

7. Read Matthew 4:4. Write in your own words what Jesus said about God's Word.

8. How can you apply Colossians 3:16?

9. Read Deuteronomy 6:6-7. What did Moses tell the people to do with God's Word?

What is a practical way you can talk about Scripture with others?

"THAT I MIGHT NOT SIN AGAINST YOU"

10. What is the Word of God able to do in your heart, according to Hebrews 4:12?

11. What results of abiding in God's Word are mentioned in John 8:31-32?

12. Read James 1:22-25. Describe the person who forgets what he sees in God's Word.

How did James say we should respond to the Word of God?

WRITE OUT PSALM 119:9,11 FROM MEMORY.

APPLYING PSALM 119:9,11

Select one of the verses you have already memorized which you need to apply this week. Now write out a prayer request based on this need.

Take a moment to pray and ask God to help you carry out your application of Scripture.

9

LOVE

Review the following verses, and check them off after quoting them correctly from memory.

- ☐ 1 John 5:11-12
- ☐ John 16:24
- ☐ 1 Corinthians 10:13
- ☐ 1 John 1:9

- ☐ Proverbs 3:5-6
- ☐ Matthew 6:33
- ☐ Philippians 4:13
- ☐ Psalm 119:9,11

MEMORIZE JOHN 13:34-35
Love

"A new command I give you: Love one another. As I have loved you, so you must love one another. By this all men will know that you are my disciples, if you love one another."

JOHN 13:34-35

What is love? John said, "This is love: not that we loved God, but that he loved us and sent his Son as an atoning sacrifice for our sins" (1 John 4:10).

God is the source of love, and also the perfect example of what love is. God *is* love.

His love is sacrificial. Christ's death is an eternal reminder of this.

God's love is also unconditional. You never have to worry about it diminishing. It is not dependent on our worthiness to receive it, for no one deserves God's love — and yet He loves everyone.

"Dear friends," John wrote, "since God so loved us, we also ought to love one another" (1 John 4:11). As you memorize John 13:34-35, think of some ways you can show God's love to others.

Exploring John 13:34-35
What is Christ's new commandment?

Whose example of love are we to follow?

What will result when Christians show one another the same kind of love Jesus extends to us?

"Love One Another"
1. What commandments does Christ emphasize in Matthew 22:37-39?

2. Read 1 John 4:7. What is the source of love?

3. Who does God love, according to John 3:16?

4. What is the result of obeying God's Word, according to 1 Peter 1:22?

How does Peter say we are to love one another?

5. Read John 15:12-13. How did Jesus demonstrate His love?

6. Read 1 John 2:5. How did John say God's love is shown in our lives?

7. From 1 John 2:6, what indicates that an individual is rightly related to Jesus Christ?

8. In Galatians 5:13, how did Paul teach Christians to exercise freedom?

9. Read 1 John 4:10 and describe God's love.

10. Read John 13:1-17. Before Jesus gave His followers a new command to love one another (John 13:34-35), how did He demonstrate His love to them?

11. Read 1 John 3:16-18. From verse 17, describe a practical way we are taught to love our brothers.

   From 1 John 3:18, describe the kind of love we should express to others.

12. Read 1 Corinthians 13. From verses 4-7, list ways you can become more loving, and use this list for prayer.

"ALL MEN WILL KNOW THAT YOU ARE MY DISCIPLES"

13. Write out John 13:35 in your own words.

WRITE OUT JOHN 13:34-35 FROM MEMORY.

APPLYING JOHN 13:34-35

Prayerfully review this chapter. Ask God to remind you of a fellow Christian to whom you need to extend more love. Then write a plan for demonstrating your love to this person this week.

10

GIVING

Review the following verses, and check them off after quoting them correctly from memory.

- ☐ 1 John 5:11-12
- ☐ John 16:24
- ☐ 1 Corinthians 10:13
- ☐ 1 John 1:9
- ☐ Proverbs 3:5-6

- ☐ Matthew 6:33
- ☐ Philippians 4:13
- ☐ Psalm 119:9,11
- ☐ John 13:34-35

MEMORIZE 2 CORINTHIANS 9:7
Giving

Each man should give what he has decided in his heart to give, not reluctantly or under compulsion, for God loves a cheerful giver.

2 CORINTHIANS 9:7

God has inexhaustible riches available for His children. We are heirs to all He possesses, for "if we are children, then we are heirs — heirs of God and co-heirs with Christ" (Romans 8:17).

God is eager to share these riches with us: "He who did not spare his own Son, but gave him up for us all — how will he not also, along with him, graciously give us all things?" (Romans 8:32).

Everything you have is from God. You can show your gratitude to

God by generously giving of yourself — your time, your possessions, your talents, and your money — to those who have needs.

Giving is sharing what God has given to us. We cannot give more than God will give back to us. Jesus said, "Give, and it will be given to you. A good measure, pressed down, shaken together and running over, will be poured into your lap. For with the measure you use, it will be measured to you" (Luke 6:38).

As you memorize 2 Corinthians 9:7, think of specific and practical ways to share with others what God has freely given you.

Exploring 2 Corinthians 9:7
What attitudes toward giving are pleasing to God?

What attitudes should you avoid?

"Each Man Should Give What He Has Decided"
1. Paraphrase 2 Corinthians 9:6.

2. What did Jesus say about spiritual treasure and material wealth in Matthew 6:19-21?

3. What warning did Jesus give in Luke 12:15?

Why do you think He issued this warning?

4. According to Acts 20:35, what did Jesus say about giving?

5. Read Matthew 6:1-4 and describe the manner of giving that God blesses.

6. Read Exodus 35:4-5. What attitude does God desire us to have as we give?

7. In 1 Chronicles 29:9, what was the people's response after they gave to God?

How had they given?

8. Read 2 Corinthians 8:9. How should Jesus' example motivate us to give liberally?

9. In 1 Corinthians 16:1-2, what plan did Paul propose for regular giving?

"GOD LOVES A CHEERFUL GIVER"
10. Read Luke 21:1-4. How did Jesus view the widow's small gift?

11. Read 2 Corinthians 9:8-15. What is promised to those who give cheerfully (verse 8)?

What will God do for generous givers (verses 10-11)?

12. From Philippians 4:18-19, list some results of giving to others.

WRITE OUT 2 CORINTHIANS 9:7 FROM MEMORY.

APPLYING 2 CORINTHIANS 9:7

What has God given you that you can share with others?

Consider your giving in the past. What is a specific way you could increase your giving to God's work or to those in need?

11

THE CHURCH

Review the following verses, and check them off after quoting them correctly from memory.

- ☐ 1 John 5:11-12
- ☐ John 16:24
- ☐ 1 Corinthians 10:13
- ☐ 1 John 1:9
- ☐ Proverbs 3:5-6

- ☐ Matthew 6:33
- ☐ Philippians 4:13
- ☐ Psalm 119:9,11
- ☐ John 13:34-35
- ☐ 2 Corinthians 9:7

MEMORIZE PSALM 122:1

The Church

I rejoiced with those who said to me, "Let us go to the house of the LORD."

PSALM 122:1

The church is made up of all true Christians everywhere — and it includes many thousands of local churches. God instituted these local churches to help Christians grow spiritually. You will have fellowship with other believers there — including opportunities to serve and encourage them. You will receive "training in righteousness" (2 Timothy 3:16) as God's Word is preached and taught in the local church.

Scripture teaches us to seek out this kind of fellowship: "Let us not give up meeting together, as some are in the habit of doing, but let us encourage one another — and all the more as you see the Day approaching" (Hebrews 10:25).

EXPLORING PSALM 122:1

What is a good attitude to have in a worship service?

What do you think made David glad as he considered going to the house of the Lord?

"I REJOICED"

1. Read Acts 2:42-47. How did the early Christians respond to the nurture and fellowship they enjoyed?

2. Why could Paul say in 1 Thessalonians 1:2-3 that he was joyful about the growth of the local church at Thessalonica?

3. In 1 Thessalonians 2:19-20, Paul again said the Thessalonian Christians made him joyful. Read 1 Thessalonians 2:13 and explain the reason for Paul's joy.

"LET US GO TO THE HOUSE OF THE LORD"

4. What did Jesus promise in Matthew 18:19-20 to those who gather in His name?

5. Paul explained one of the church's main purposes in Ephesians 4:11-12. Write out these verses in your own words.

6. Read Ephesians 4:13-15. What will be the result in our lives when the church's ministry follows the pattern described in Ephesians 4:11-12?

7. According to Ephesians 4:11-15, who in addition to the pastor is responsible for the growth of Christians in a local congregation?

   According to Ephesians 4:15-16, how is the body of Christ built up?

8. In 1 Thessalonians 5:12-13, how did Paul say we should regard our Christian leaders?

   How should we follow the example of our spiritual leaders, according to Hebrews 13:7?

9. Read Colossians 1:13-20. Who is the head of the church?

How did Paul describe the church in Colossians 1:18?

10. What is the result of hearing God's Word proclaimed, according to Romans 10:17?

11. Read Romans 12:3-16. Summarize what this passage teaches about relationships within the body of Christ.

12. What did Paul long for among the Christians at Rome, according to Romans 15:5-6?

13. What did Jesus especially pray for all believers in John 17:20-23?

WRITE OUT PSALM 122:1 FROM MEMORY.

APPLYING PSALM 122:1

Prayerfully review your study, especially the Scripture passages and ideas which were most helpful to you personally. Write a short paragraph on why the church is important to your spiritual growth.

How can you better serve your local church?

12

GOOD WORKS

Review the following verses, and check them off after quoting them correctly from memory.

☐ 1 John 5:11-12
☐ John 16:24
☐ 1 Corinthians 10:13
☐ 1 John 1:9
☐ Proverbs 3:5-6
☐ Matthew 6:33

☐ Philippians 4:13
☐ Psalm 119:9,11
☐ John 13:34-35
☐ 2 Corinthians 9:7
☐ Psalm 122:1

MEMORIZE EPHESIANS 2:10
Good Works

For we are God's workmanship, created in Christ Jesus to do good works, which God prepared in advance for us to do.

EPHESIANS 2:10

Your salvation wasn't earned by your good deeds. We are all saved by faith, and not by good works (see Ephesians 2:8-9). Nevertheless, God wants your life now to be filled with good works — doing what is right and helpful to others. In this we are to follow the example of Jesus, who "went around doing good" (Acts 10:38).

It is faith alone that saves, but the faith that saves is never alone.

Paul wrote that believers should be "careful to devote themselves to doing what is good. These things are excellent and profitable for everyone" (Titus 3:8). As you seek to do God's will through good works, you — and others through you — will profit. And God will be glorified, because He has good works planned especially for you to accomplish.

EXPLORING EPHESIANS 2:10
What do you think "God's workmanship" means?

What are we created for?

What are good works?

"FOR WE ARE GOD'S WORKMANSHIP"
1. Read Titus 3:8. Who should do good works?

   Who should benefit from good works?

2. According to Ephesians 2:8-9, why don't good works have a part in our salvation?

3. Paraphrase Titus 3:14.

4. What should be the result of our good works, according to Matthew 5:14-16?

5. Read Colossians 3:17. As we do good works, who do we represent?

"To Do Good Works"

6. What were the following Christians commended for?
   Dorcas (Acts 9:36)

   Phoebe (Romans 16:1-2)

   Epaphras (Colossians 4:12)

7. Read Matthew 25:31-46. List several practical ways in which you can serve Christ by doing good to others.

8. In 1 Peter 2:12, what did Peter say would make non-Christians glorify God?

9. To whom should we do good, according to Galatians 6:10?

10. What ways for doing good are mentioned in the following passages?
Romans 12:13

2 Corinthians 9:7-8

James 1:27

11. In James 2:15-16, what did James say proves our true concern for those in need?

12. Read 2 Timothy 3:16-17. What equips a Christian for every good work?

WRITE OUT EPHESIANS 2:10 FROM MEMORY.

APPLYING EPHESIANS 2:10
Prayerfully review your study and list several practical good works you could do for someone.

Now write the name of one person for whom you would like to do a good work this week, and circle in your list above the thing you would like to do for this person.

13

WITNESSING

Review the following verses, and check them off after quoting them correctly from memory.

- ☐ 1 John 5:11-12
- ☐ John 16:24
- ☐ 1 Corinthians 10:13
- ☐ 1 John 1:9
- ☐ Proverbs 3:5-6
- ☐ Matthew 6:33

- ☐ Philippians 4:13
- ☐ Psalm 119:9,11
- ☐ John 13:34-35
- ☐ 2 Corinthians 9:7
- ☐ Psalm 122:1
- ☐ Ephesians 2:10

MEMORIZE MARK 5:19

Witnessing

"Go home to your family and tell them how much the Lord has done for you, and how he has had mercy on you."

MARK 5:19

What could you tell someone about how your life has changed because of Christ? Have you thought about how to give a clear explanation of your faith?

Peter wrote, "Always be prepared to give an answer to everyone who asks you to give the reason for the hope that you have" (1 Peter 3:15).

As someone who has experienced God's saving love, you have much to share.

In Mark 5 we read how Jesus encountered a man who was demon-possessed and living in tombs. With power Jesus healed the man.

As Jesus was leaving, the man begged Him to let him come along. Jesus' reply — the memory verse for this lesson — was that the man should instead return home and share his newfound life with others. The man did so, and we read in Mark 5:20 that "all the people were amazed."

We too were living in the "tombs" of deadly sin before we accepted Christ as our Savior. And so we also have good news to tell others!

Exploring Mark 5:19
What did Jesus tell this man to share with members of his family?

Read Mark 5:2-5 and 5:15. What impact do you think this man's changed life would have on his family?

"Tell Them How Much the Lord Has Done for You"
1. Read 2 Corinthians 5:20. What does God say we are?

2. In Acts 4:18-20, Peter and John were ordered not to speak or teach in the name of Jesus. Why did Peter and John say they could not obey this order (verse 20)?

3. Write a paragraph summarizing the most important things you believe the Lord has done for you.

4. Read Romans 1:16. Why can we have confidence in speaking to others about the good news of Jesus Christ?

"Tell Them . . . How He Has Had Mercy on You"

5. What important facts do you see in these verses about why and how God saved you?

Romans 3:23

Romans 6:23

Romans 5:8

John 1:12

6. Describe in your own words the truth of Romans 5:1 as you have experienced it in your life.

7. How did Paul summarize the gospel in 1 Corinthians 15:3-4?

8. You are sure to receive a variety of responses as you share your faith with others. Many will raise objections to the gospel and will not recognize their need of Christ. Read the Scriptures listed below and tell how they apply to the following objections to the gospel:

"I'm basically a good person." (Ephesians 2:8-9; Titus 3:5)

"People from all religions will make it to heaven." (John 14:6; Acts 4:12)

"What about all the Christians I know who are hypocrites?" (Romans 14:12)

"I'll become a Christian someday." (2 Corinthians 6:2; James 4:14)

9. What did Paul request prayer for regarding his witnessing to others (see Colossians 4:3-4)?

WRITE OUT MARK 5:19 FROM MEMORY.

APPLYING MARK 5:19

Write here the names of some people you would like to witness to about what Christ has done for you.

Begin to pray regularly for these people, and plan a time you could share the gospel with at least one of them. Briefly describe your plan here.

CHECK OUT THESE OTHER GREAT STUDIES FROM NAVPRESS!

Lessons on Assurance
The Navigators

978-0-89109-160-8
Basic Bible studies on five beginning principles for following Christ, plus five corresponding Scripture memory verses titled *Beginning with Christ*.

Lessons on Christian Living
The Navigators

978-0-89109-162-2
Bible studies on eight more principles for Christian growth, plus eight Scripture memory verses titled *Going On with Christ*.

To order copies, call NavPress at 1-800-366-7788 or log on to www.navpress.com.

Discipleship Inside Out™